Celebrated Piano Solos 2

Ten Diverse Solos for Late Elementary to Early Intermediate Pianists
(UK Exam Grades 1 & 2)

Robert D. Vandall

I always appreciate a supplemental solo book that provides musical variety for my students. These solos, many of which have been chosen for local and national festivals, represent many different styles, moods, keys, meter signatures, tempos, and pianistic techniques. Skip around in this collection and follow your students' interests, celebrating the diversity of their musical tastes and the variety this collection provides for them!

Robert D. Vandall

Contents

Alfred

Courtly Dance

Robert D. Vandall

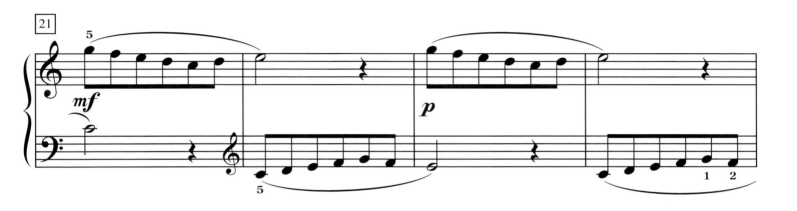

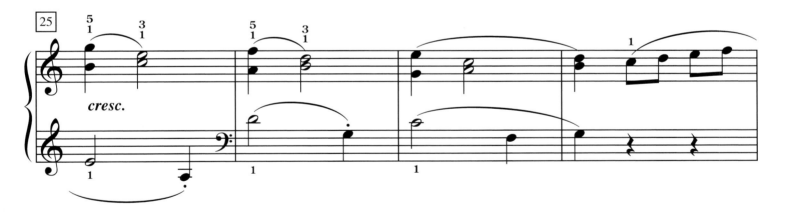

D. C. al Fine

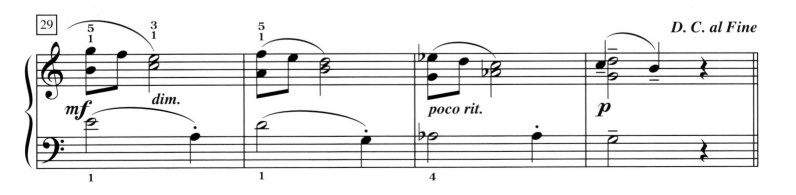

Crooked Run Rag

Robert D. Vandall

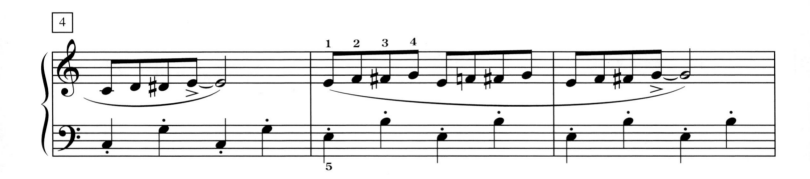

Antique Toccata

Robert D. Vandall

Carousel

Robert D. Vandall

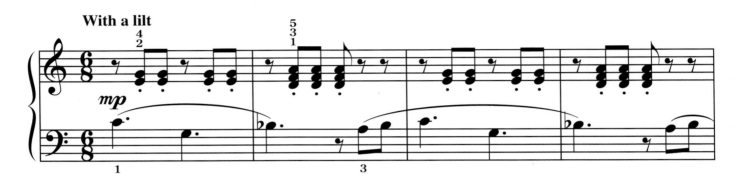

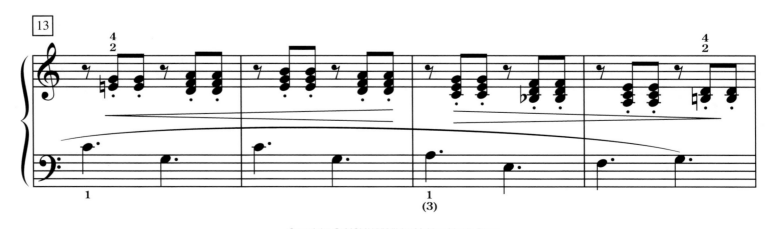

Pianist on the Prowl

Robert D. Vandall

LH one octave lower throughout

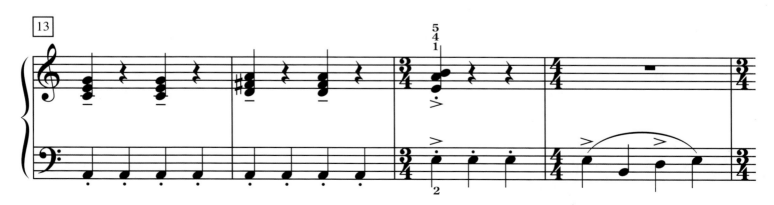

Touch and Go

Robert D. Vandall

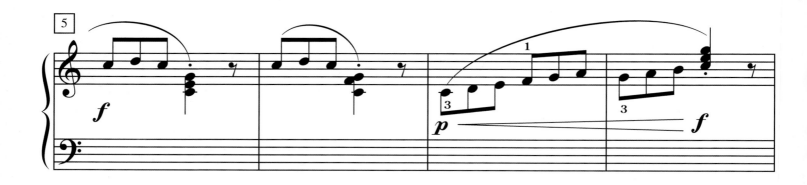

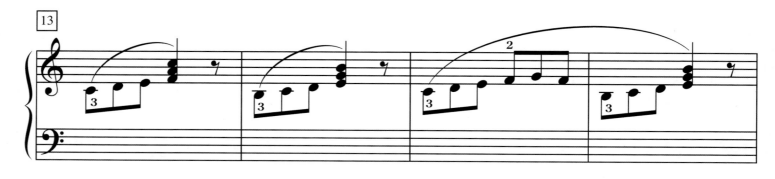

Grandma's Ginger Cookies

Robert D. Vandall

LH one octave lower than written throughout

Best Friends

Robert D. Vandall

In a Jam

Robert D. Vandall

Moderate tempo; well-accented

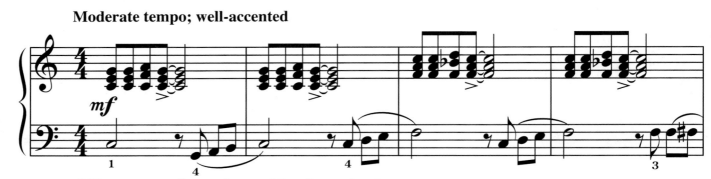

LH one octave lower than written throughout

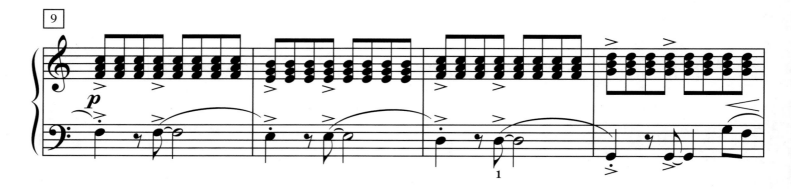

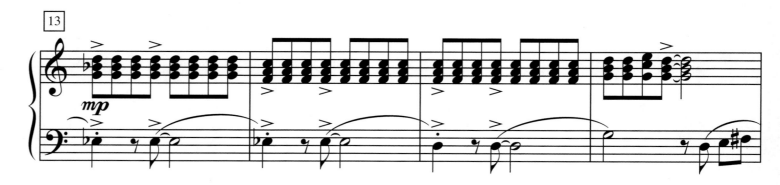

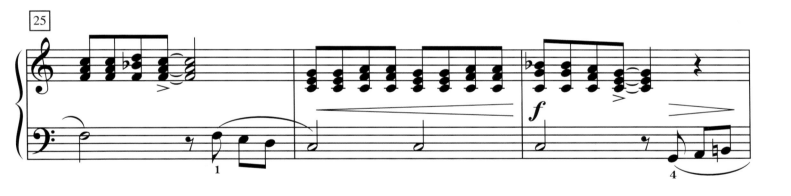

High Street Stomp

Robert D. Vandall

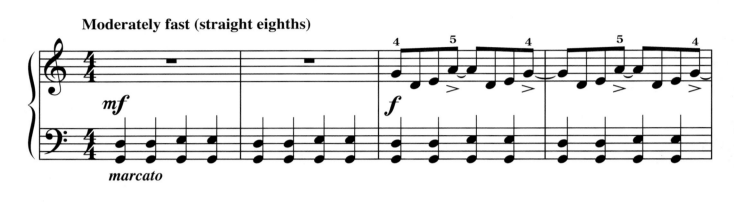

8va